PHILIPPIANS:
DISPENSATIONALLY CONSIDERED

A GRACE EXPOSITIONAL COMMENTARY

SECOND EDITION

Dr. David Alan Greene

GraceWord Publishing, LLC
www.gracewordpublishing.com
U.S.A.

Contents

Acknowledgements   ix

Introduction   xi

Chapter 1:   Paul's Visit To Philippi   1

Chapter 2:   Philippians 1   11

Chapter 3:   Philippians 2   25

Chapter 4:   Philippians 3   41

Chapter 5:   Philippians 4   57

Epilogue   71

Other GraceWord Publications   85

About The Author   87

To My Son Matthew

Whatsoever things are true,
whatsoever things are honest,
whatsoever things are just,
whatsoever things are pure,
whatsoever things are lovely,
whatsoever things are of good report;
if there be any virtue,
and if there be any praise,
think on these things.

- The Apostle Paul

Acknowledgements

A special thank you for the support and encouragement from Jon and Susan McMahan. To Winnie Stearns and Frances Greene who worked to proof-read the manuscript, my gratitude.

x

Introduction

It would be a great disservice to some readers, those new to the concept of right division, to jump right into studying the book of Philippians. Those readers will benefit by covering some preliminary ground. The letter to the Philippians is one of thirteen letters or epistles written by the Apostle Paul. Nine of these epistles were written to assemblies of grace believers. Four were written to individuals and are known as the pastoral epistles. These included two letters to Timothy, and one to Titus and Philemon. All of these letters, with the exception of Romans, were written to people Paul had visited personally. He had lived with many of them and taught them face to face. Therefore, the groups who received these letters were familiar with Paul's teaching before receiving his letter. Since this is the case, it may leave you, the reader, at a disadvantage unless you are also familiar with his teaching.

From the beginning, it is important that one not confuse Paul's Gospel of Grace with the Gospel of

The Kingdom taught by the other apostles. The book of Romans is different from the others. It is placed first in the series of his epistles. Some of those who had heard Paul teach personally had relocated to the capitol city of Rome. Many others there had not met or heard him teach. They had become believers through the testimony of others. It is for that reason that Romans is the definitive book of Pauline doctrine because it is a summary of Paul's teachings. It was written to provide new believers with a comprehensive foundation of doctrine. It is upon this doctrine that all his other letters were written.

Sometimes I use as an example the multi-part series of an epic story like Star Wars. Think how difficult it would be to understand the full extent of the story by starting in the middle. Therefore, I would like to provide you with a brief summary of the revelation received by the Apostle Paul. He made three missionary trips. His last trip would be to Rome where he would be executed. He wrote the letter to the Philippians from Ephesus or from Rome while a prisoner awaiting trial.

Scripture will show that the Apostle Paul was given a unique gospel message by the Risen Savior. It had remained a mystery from the beginning of time until it was disclosed to Paul by Jesus Christ.

This gospel message was specifically directed to the Gentiles. The Bible states this multiple times. Notice how God directs Ananias to heal Paul's blindness which resulted from his confrontation on the Road to Damascus. Acts 9:3-9:

> 3 And as he journeyed, he came near Damascus: and suddenly there shined round about him a light from heaven:
> 4 And he fell to the earth, and heard a voice saying unto him, Saul, Saul, why persecutest thou me? 5 And he said, Who art thou, Lord? And the Lord said, I am Jesus whom thou persecutest: it is hard for thee to kick against the pricks.
>
> 6 And he trembling and astonished said, Lord, what wilt thou have me to do? And the Lord said unto him, Arise, and go into the city, and it shall be told thee what thou must do. 7 And the men which journeyed with him stood speechless, hearing a voice, but seeing no man. 8 And Saul arose from the earth; and when his eyes were opened, he saw no man: but they led him by the hand, and brought him into Damascus. 9 And he was three days without sight, and neither did eat nor drink.

It is important to know that the Apostle Paul never met Jesus during His earthly ministry. Therefore, he could not fulfill the requirements for the replacement of Judas as the twelfth apostle (See Acts 1:21-26).

Pay close attention to this dialogue between God and Ananias. Acts 9:10-12

> 10 **And there was a certain disciple at Damascus, named Ananias; and to him said the Lord in a vision, Ananias. And he said, Behold, I am here, Lord.** 11 **And the Lord said unto him, Arise, and go into the street which is called Straight, and enquire in the house of Judas for one called Saul, of Tarsus: for, behold, he prayeth,** 12 **And hath seen in a vision a man named Ananias coming in, and putting his hand on him, that he might receive his sight.**

The above event occurred after the stoning of Stephen. The complete story can be found in Acts 6 and 7. Paul, at that time called Saul, consented to Stephen's death, but sought to arrest these new believers and bring them to Jerusalem for judgement and possible death. Can you imagine Jesus being interested in this persecutor of His Church? The news was well known locally, and Ananias was understandably hesitant. Verses 13-16:

> 13 Then Ananias answered, Lord, I have heard by many of this man, how much evil he hath done to thy saints at Jerusalem: 14 And here he hath authority from the chief priests to bind all that call on thy name. 15 But the Lord said unto him, <u>Go thy way: for he is a chosen vessel unto me, to bear my name before the Gentiles, and kings, and the children of Israel:</u> 16 For I will shew him how great things he must suffer for my name's sake.

Never before had Jesus directed His apostles to go to the Gentiles. The Law required Jews to remain separate from the Gentiles. We see that, during His earthly ministry, Jesus dispatched His Twelve to the Jews. He gave them a different gospel message than the one He would later give Paul. Matthew 10:5-7:

> 5 These twelve Jesus sent forth, and commanded them, saying, <u>Go not into the way of the Gentiles</u>, and into any city of the Samaritans enter ye not: 6 <u>But go rather to the lost sheep of the house of Israel.</u> 7 And as ye go, preach, saying, The kingdom of heaven is at hand.

He specifically directed the Twelve to go to *the lost sheep of the house of Israel.*

In Paul's letter to the Galatians, he explains something. He most likely shared this with other believers while he was with them in person. The verses below recall his second meeting with the other apostles in Jerusalem. Only once before had Paul met Peter and James on a previous trip. This records his second trip to meet with them. Galatians 2:1-9

> 1 **Then fourteen years after I went up again to Jerusalem with Barnabas, and took Titus with me also. 2 And I went up by revelation, and communicated unto them that gospel which I preach among the Gentiles, but privately to them which were of reputation, lest by any means I should run, or had run, in vain.**
>
> 3 **But neither Titus, who was with me, being a Greek, was compelled to be circumcised: 4 And that because of false brethren unawares brought in, who came in privily to spy out our liberty which we have in Christ Jesus, that they might bring us into bondage:**
>
> 5 **To whom we gave place by subjection,**

no, not for an hour; that the truth of the gospel might continue with you. 6 But of these who seemed to be somewhat [of importance], (whatsoever they were, it maketh no matter to me: God accepteth no man's person:) for they who seemed to be somewhat in conference added nothing to me:

7 But contrariwise, when they saw that <u>the gospel of the uncircumcision</u> was committed unto me, as <u>the gospel of the circumcision</u> was unto Peter; 8 (For he that wrought effectually in Peter to the apostleship of the circumcision, the same was mighty in me toward the Gentiles:)

9 And when James, Cephas, and John, who seemed to be pillars, perceived the grace that was given unto me, they gave to me and Barnabas the right hands of fellowship; that <u>we should go unto the heathen,</u> and <u>they unto the circumcision.</u>

This meeting took place prior to his writing to the Philippians.

In a letter to the Corinthians, Paul provides a concise statement of his gospel. Notice his use of the definite article "the" when referring to *the* gospel "wherein" they stood — in other words, the basis of their faith. Note its simplicity! 1 Corinthians 15:1-4:

> 1 **Moreover, brethren, I declare unto you the gospel which I preached unto you, which also ye have received, and wherein ye stand; 2 By which also ye are saved, if ye keep in memory what I preached unto you, unless ye have believed in vain.**
>
> 3 **For I delivered unto you first of all that which I also received, [1] how that Christ died for our sins according to the scriptures; 4 [2] And that he was buried, and [3] that he rose again the third day according to the scriptures:**

The gospel consists of (1) Christ's death on the Cross, (2) His burial, and (3) His resurrection. According to Paul's teaching, our belief in this *gospel* is all we need for our salvation. This leaves nothing else for us to do. Jesus Christ accomplished it all! We receive it by *faith* – by *believing* God's Word.

Paul makes clear the sufficiency of Christ's

completed work on the Cross. He does this by reminding us that nothing else can be added. This is perhaps one of the most quoted of Paul's verses. Ephesians 2:8-9:

> 8 **For by grace are ye saved through faith**; and that not of yourselves: it is the gift of God: 9 **Not of works, lest any man should boast.**

In Galatians he chastised some of the grace believers for adding other requirements for salvation beyond what the Savior had already finished. Unfortunately, many churches still teach today the need for works. Paul's gospel message is different from that of the Twelve. Most Christian are taught, contrary to Scripture, there is only one message of good news. The truth will be substantiated by the God's Word.

In Galatians 1, Paul states he neither received his gospel message from the other apostles nor from any other man. If that is the case, then where did he receive it? He testifies that he received it directly from the Risen Savior. Galatians 1:11-12:

> 11 **But I certify you, brethren, that the gospel which was preached of me is not after [from] man. 12 For I neither received it of [by] man, neither was I**

taught it, but by the revelation of Jesus Christ.

Why Paul? I asked my Methodist pastor, when I was growing up, why he did not preach from Paul's letters. He told me that it was because Paul had persecuted the Church. This is the same reason that most have shunned him throughout history.

Paul gives his view on this. Verses 13-17:

13 **For ye have heard of my conversation [manner of living] in time past in the Jews' religion, how that beyond measure I persecuted the church of God, and wasted it:** 14 **And profited [advanced] in the Jews' religion above many my equals in mine own nation, being more exceedingly zealous of the traditions of my fathers.**

15 **But <u>when it pleased God</u>, who separated me from my mother's womb, and called me by his grace,** 16 **<u>To reveal his Son in [to] me</u>, that I might preach him among the heathen[Gentiles]; <u>immediately I conferred not with flesh and blood</u> [any man]:** 17 **Neither went I up to Jerusalem to them which were apostles**

before me; but [instead] I went into Arabia, and [later] returned again unto Damascus.

God set Paul a part for a special ministry to the Gentiles. That did not mean that the offer of the Gospel of Grace was not also open to the Jews. It is available to everyone but effective for only those who choose to believe. Paul refers to this many times throughout his epistles.

Here is an important point I would like to make. This will help those new to this whole concept that Paul is different from the other writers of Scripture. Find a large jumbo paper clip. Now, beginning with the last page of Acts and going to the first page of Hebrews place the paper clip over the pages in between. By doing this, the books contained within the paper clip should start with Romans and end with Philemon. These are the thirteen epistles written by Paul. This is a visual representation.

If we look at the last chapter of Acts, immediately before Paul's first book, then we will find a meeting recorded there. It happened while Paul was incarcerated in Rome. He called the local Jewish leaders to meet with him. (See Acts 28:16-30.) After reasoning with them at great length, they left not convinced but debating among themselves. Here we see that Paul makes a proclamation, a verbal pro-nouncement. Acts 28:28:

28 Be it known therefore unto you, that the salvation of God is sent unto the Gentiles, and that they will hear it.

There were only two groups of people. There were the Jews, God's chosen people, and there were non-Jews–the Gentiles. This proclamation by Paul imme-diately precedes his first epistle. Now, let us go to the other side of the paper clip.

The first book which follows Paul's epistles is the book of Hebrews. Can you see the pattern here? The message Paul received from God is directed to the Gentiles. It is called the Gospel of Grace. The word *grace* means *gift*. *Faith* means *believing* what someone said. Therefore, salvation by faith means believing God is graciously offering salvation as a *gift* to all who will *believe* it. This is only possible be-cause Christ paid the price in full!

Here is a story for you. The epistles which fol-low after Paul's epistles are called the Hebrew epis-tles. They are the book of Hebrews and those that fol-low. I was teaching a Bible study and explaining sal-vation by grace through faith. Someone interrupted me, "Hey, wait a minute! What about faith without works is dead?!" He was speaking about the verses in James. So, I had everyone turn to these verses and I read them aloud. James 2:18-20:

> 18 **Yea, a man may say, Thou hast faith, and I have works: shew me thy faith without thy works, and I will shew thee my faith by my works. 19 Thou believest that there is one God; thou doest well: the devils also believe, and tremble. 20 But wilt thou know, O vain man, that <u>faith without works is dead?</u>**

I confirmed these were the verses to which he was referring. Then, I directed the group to turn to the beginning of the book of James. These verses I also read aloud. James 1:1:

> 1 **James, a servant of God and of the Lord Jesus Christ, <u>to the twelve tribes which are scattered abroad</u>, greeting.**

James is writing to the twelve tribes of Israel scattered throughout the earth. I asked him, "Which tribe are you from?" In other words, James is writing to the children of Israel — *the twelve tribes which are scattered* amongst the other nations. All the books in the Bible that follow Paul's epistles, beginning with Hebrews, are written to Israel and not the Gentiles!

GraceWord Publishing has a list of excellent books explaining this in greater detail listed in the back of this book. One book, entitled Letters to Theophilus, is a summary of the entire Bible from Genesis to Revelation. It provides an understanding of the Bible's framework. In addition to GraceWord, there are online resources. This includes Grace Bible Network and the Berean Bible Society. When I was first introduced to rightly dividing the Word of Truth, I watched Les Feldick, a mid-west rancher, who has taught many people to understand and enjoy their Bibles. He has many YouTube® videos and TV programs. Les is with the Lord now. However, his 30-minute Bible classes are still worth watching. Look for the program: Through The Bible With Les Feldick.

With this introduction to Paul and his unique gospel message, we are ready to begin our study of his letter to the grace believers in the Philippian assembly.

1

Paul's Visit To Philippi

Philippi is a city located in Macedonia which is in the northern part of what is now Greece. It was the first city in Europe that Paul would visit and establish a community of grace believers. We have an historical account of this visit recorded by Luke in the Acts of the Apostles. Acts 16:6-9:

> 6 **Now when they had gone throughout Phrygia and the region of Galatia, and were forbidden of the Holy Ghost to preach the word in Asia,**

> 7 **After they were come to Mysia, they assayed [reasoned] to go into Bithynia: but the Spirit suffered [allowed] them not.** 8 **And they passing by Mysia came down to Troas.**

9 And a vision appeared to Paul in the night; There stood a man of Macedonia, and prayed [requested] him, saying, <u>Come over into Macedonia, and help us.</u>

Philippi is located in Macedonia. Paul had traveled through Asia Minor which is now present-day Turkey. God was calling him towards Europe.

Upon receiving this request in his dream, Paul responds. Acts 16:10-12:

10 And after he had seen the vision, immediately we endeavoured to go into Macedonia, assuredly gathering [believing] that the Lord had called us for to preach the gospel unto them.

11 Therefore loosing from [leaving] Troas, we came with a straight course to Samothracia, and the next day to Neapolis; 12 And from thence to Philippi, which is the chief city of that part of Macedonia, and a colony . . .

They soon arrived in the city of Philippi. Once there, they began to make known the Gospel of Grace. Verses 12-13:

12 . . . and we were in that city abiding certain days. **13** And on the sabbath we went out of the city by a river side, where prayer was wont [accustomed] to be made; and we sat down, and spake unto the women which resorted [frequented] thither [there].

Being visitors in a foreign land, God provided for their needs through a local woman who sold luxurious fabric dyed purple. The dye came from certain snails taken from the Mediterranean Sea. When boiled, they ejected a purplish dye. Acts 16:14:

14 And a certain woman named Lydia, a seller of purple, of the city of Thyatira, which worshipped God, heard us: whose heart the Lord opened, that she attended [listened] unto the things which were spoken of [by] Paul.

Lydia listened to Paul's teaching. She, along with those in her household, believed. We will see that baptism is practiced by Paul only during his early ministry. Baptism was a public acknowledgement of faith. Later, he stops doing this. Baptism is a requirement of the Gospel of the Kingdom preached by Peter. "Repent, and be baptized every one of you in the name of Jesus Christ for the remission of sins"

(Acts 2:38). Verse 15:

> 15 And when she was baptized, and her household, she besought us, saying, If ye have judged me to be faithful to the Lord, come into my house, and abide there. And she constrained [urged] us.

Her argument was compelling. In other words, "she wouldn't take no for an answer" that they should come and stay as her guests.

There was another woman there who had a demonic influence upon her. Verses 16-18:

> 16 And it came to pass, as we went to prayer, a certain damsel [young woman] possessed with a spirit of divination met us, which brought her masters much gain by soothsaying [foretelling]:
>
> 17 The same followed Paul and us, and cried, saying, These men are the servants of the most high God, which shew unto us the way of salvation.
>
> 18 And this did she many days. But Paul, being grieved, [he] turned and said to the spirit, I command thee in the name

**of Jesus Christ to come out of her. And
he [the spirit] came out the same hour.**

Consider the interruption this young woman had on
Paul's ministry. The spirit which possessed her rec-
ognized Paul as a messenger of God. To end this con-
stant annoyance, he commanded that the spirit leave
her, and it did. Verses 19-21:

> 19 **And when her masters saw that the
> hope of their gains [profits] was gone,
> they caught Paul and Silas, and drew
> them into the marketplace unto the rul-
> ers, 20 And brought them to the magis-
> trates, saying, These men, being Jews,
> do exceedingly trouble our city, 21 And
> teach customs, which are not lawful for
> us to receive, neither to observe, being
> Romans.**

Both Paul and Silas were grabbed by these
profiteers of the occult, They brought them before
the magistrates of the city. The charge was that these
men were teaching what was not lawful or approved
for Romans to hear or believe. Common Law which
applies laws equally without discrimination. Civil
Law originated from Roman Law and is adminis-
tered by magistrates on a case-by-case basis. In view
of the agitated crowd, they made what they believed

to be a politically correct decision. Verses 22-24:

> **22 And the multitude rose up together against them: and the magistrates rent off [tore] their clothes, and commanded to beat them.**
>
> **23 And when they had laid many stripes upon them, they cast them into prison, charging the jailor to keep them safely: 24 Who, having received such a charge, thrust them into the inner prison, and made their feet fast in the stocks.**

Paul and Silas now found themselves in the most secure cell deep within the jail. Being confined and prevented the freedom of movement, what was their response? Verses 25-26:

> **25 And at midnight Paul and Silas prayed, and sang praises unto God: and the prisoners heard them. 26 And suddenly there was a great earthquake, so that the foundations of the prison were shaken: and immediately all the doors were opened, and every one's bands were loosed [undone].**

The jailor, being an officer of the Roman court, was

entrusted with the responsibility of his prisoners. He was under peril of life should his charges escape. Knowing this will help make sense of his response in verse 27:

> 27 **And the keeper of the prison awaking out of his sleep, and seeing the prison doors open, he drew out his sword, and would have killed himself, supposing that the prisoners had been fled.**

Paul immediately stopped him from killing himself. Verses 28-29:

> 28 **But Paul cried with a loud voice, saying, Do thyself no harm: for we are all here. 29 Then he called for a light, and sprang in, and came trembling, and fell down before Paul and Silas,**

Realizing this, the jailor was amazed that no one had taken advantage of the situation to gain their freedom. The other prisoners, I am sure, were amazed by this miraculous event as well. They had heard Paul praying, thanking God, and rejoicing with songs just prior to the earthquake. Since he must still account for all his prisoners, the jailor brought them out into the open. There he asked Paul and Silas about salvation. Verse 30:

30 And [the jailor] brought them out, and said, Sirs, what must I do to be saved?

The Lord provides us all with openings to share the Gospel of Grace with others. It may not be the result of such a miraculous event as this, but the opportunities are there. Paul takes this opportunity to teach. Verses 31-34:

31 And they said, Believe on the Lord Jesus Christ, and thou shalt be saved, and thy house. 32 And they spake unto him [the jailor] the word of the Lord, and to all that were in his house.

33 And he [the jailor] took them the same hour of the night, and washed their stripes; and was baptized, he and all his, straightway. 34 And when he had brought them into his house, he set meat before them, and rejoiced, believing in God with all his house.

What a wonderful turn of events. Having witnessed the working of God and His graciousness towards him, the jailor was saved along with his family. Perhaps it was upon this event that Paul reflected when he wrote in Romans 8:28:

28 And we know that all things work together for good to them that love God, to them who are the called according to his purpose.

The next day, the magistrates, having met the expectations of the mob, decided to let Paul and Silas go. Although their belief was these men were troublesome Jews, they were, in fact, Roman citizens whom they had beaten. Acts 16:35-37:

35 And when it was day, the magistrates sent the serjeants, saying, Let those men go. 36 And the keeper of the prison told this saying to Paul, The magistrates have sent to let you go: now therefore depart, and go in peace.

37 But Paul said unto them, They have beaten us openly uncondemned, being Romans, and have cast us into prison; and now do they thrust us out privily? nay verily; but let them come themselves and fetch us out.

This was a grave offense to Rome. The message the sergeant-at-arms brought to the magistrates was, understandably, worrisome. Verses 38-39:

38 And the serjeants told these words unto the magistrates: and they feared, when they heard that they were Romans. 39 And they came and besought them, and brought them out, and desired them to depart out of the city.

Having dealt shamefully with these two Roman citizens, the magistrates, I am sure, were humbled. Following this event, Paul and Silas did not leave but instead fellowshipped with other grace believers at Lydia's home before leaving. Verse 40:

40 And they went out of the prison, and entered into the house of Lydia: and when they had seen the brethren, they comforted them, and departed.

It is to these grace believers that Paul is writing this letter.

2

Philippians 1

Paul wrote this letter to the Philippians either while he was in Ephesus or, more probably, while he was a prisoner in Rome about 62 A.D. This places it towards the end of his life. Some theologians date his death between 62 to 64 A.D. The letter includes instruction on unity of the body of believers and humility for believers. The Philippians continued to be a source of joy and encouragement for Paul throughout his ministry. He rejoices at their continuing progress in the gospel and expresses his gratitude to the Philippians for their support. They, like Paul, faced many hardships for their faith. The tone of the letter reveals his close personal relationship with this group of grace believers.

He begins with a greeting. As is his usual practice befitting his apostleship of the Gospel of Grace, he includes in his greeting the words *grace* and *peace*.

We are presently under *grace* in this present dispensation. During this Age of Grace, God is offering amnesty as a gift to all. However, this gift will only be effective for those who choose to believe and accept His offer. Therefore, God is currently at *peace* with all people until He withdraws His offer of salvation by grace through faith alone. Philippians 1:1-2:

> **1 Paul and Timotheus, the servants of Jesus Christ, to all the saints in Christ Jesus which are at Philippi, with the bishops and deacons: 2 Grace be unto you, and peace, from God our Father, and from the Lord Jesus Christ.**

Since his initial visit, the grace believers in Philippi continued to be an encouragement to Paul. There is nothing more gratifying to teachers than to see their students understand and effectively put into practice what Paul taught. He remembers them often in his prayers. Verses 3-5:

> **3 I thank my God upon every remembrance of you, 4 Always in every prayer of mine for you all making request with joy, 5 For your fellowship in the gospel from the first day until now;**

These grace believers were committed to living according to the Gospel of Grace.

He tells them of his confidence in the depth of their commitment. The works which the Lord had begun in them, like fruit, will continue until *the day of Jesus Christ*. This is a reference used elsewhere in Paul's writing. It is the day for which all grace believers eagerly await—the day of *His calling*. It is also known as the Rapture. This is the day when He will call all grace believers unto Himself. Verse 6:

> **6 Being confident of this very thing, that he which hath begun a good work in you will perform it <u>until the day of Jesus Christ</u>:**

In the next verse, the word *meet* means *suitable or proper*. He is confident in their salvation from the good works *the Lord produces from them*. Whether in the bonds in prison or being bound to the gospel message, both defending and advancing it, the Philippians share in his grace. Verse 7:

> **7 Even as it is meet for me to think this of you all, because I have you in my heart; inasmuch as both in my bonds, and in the defence and confirmation of the gospel, ye all are partakers of my grace.**

Paul often calls upon God to be his witness because of his close relationship with Him and as a witness to his work. The word *bowels* means *the innermost part, the heart, or the very core* of a being. Verse 8:

> 8 **For God is my record, how greatly I long after you all in the bowels of Jesus Christ.**

Paul prays earnestly from the depths of his being for these grace believers in Philippi. Verses 9-10:

> 9 **And this I pray, that your love may abound yet more and more in knowledge and in all judgment; 10 That ye may approve things that are excellent; that ye may be sincere and without offence <u>till the day of Christ</u>;**

There is the reference to the *day of Jesus Christ*. Is there anything more important to believers today than the assurance of *His Calling?* This prayer is similar to what he prayed for the Ephesians. To the same end, he wanted them to grow in wisdom and knowledge of the Word of God. Ephesians 1:16-18:

> 16 **[I] Cease not to give thanks for you, making mention of you in my prayers;**

17 That the God of our Lord Jesus Christ, the Father of glory, may give unto you the spirit of wisdom and revelation in the knowledge of him:

18 The eyes of your understanding being enlightened; <u>that ye may know what is the hope of his calling</u>, and what the riches of the glory of his inheritance in the saints,

Here is another reference to *His Calling*. Paul is writing of *His Calling* of grace believers unto Himself–the Rapture. I know I am being repetitive, but this is a critical point in the future of those saved by grace.

It is possible to measure the depth of someone's relationship with God and His Son. One only has to look at their relationship with the Word of God. Paul continues by describing the natural outflow from such a relationship whereby Christ Himself bears fruit in us. Philippians 1:11:

11 Being filled with the fruits of righteousness, which are by [from] Jesus Christ, unto the glory and praise of God.

Who is the Source of the fruits of righteousness?

They are from Jesus Christ. Let us compare this to Ephesians. This verse follows one of the most quoted verses which I include. Ephesians 2:8-10:

> 8 **For by grace are ye saved through faith; and that not of yourselves: it is the gift of God:** 9 **Not of works, lest any man should boast.**
>
> 10 <u>**For we are his workmanship, created in Christ Jesus unto good works, which God hath before ordained that we should walk in them.**</u>

From the depth of our understanding God's Word, and our relationship with Jesus Christ, we learn that it is He Who bears the *fruits of righteousness* in us. We are saved by grace through faith and not by works. We know this. We know that our salvation is secure because His Spirit dwells in us. Therefore, our good works are not done to achieve salvation but are a testament to His righteousness that dwells within us!

Returning to our text, we find Paul sharing with his friends some of his personal hardships. Philippians 1:12-14:

> 12 **But I would [that] ye should understand, brethren, that the things which**

**happened unto me have fallen out ra-
ther unto the furtherance of the gospel;**

**13 So that my bonds in Christ are mani-
fest [made known] in all the palace, and
in all other places; 14 And many of the
brethren in the Lord, waxing [growing]
confident by my bonds, are much more
bold to speak the word without fear.**

His conversation or life became a living example of
or testimony for God. Others saw this and it became
an encouragement to others who grow confident and
preach the Word of God more boldly.

In his letter to grace believers in Rome, he
makes this same point. Paul tells them what was in-
tended to be an obstacle and hinder believers would
be transformed into good. Romans 8:28:

**28 And we know that all things work to-
gether for good to them that love God,
to them who are the called according to
his purpose.**

Everything, both the bad and the good, work together to benefit those who love God and are *called
according to His purpose*. As an apostle, Paul was
called according to God's purpose and his life is a

testimony to this.

Friend, I would like to ask you to stop for a moment. If you are like most people, then you have worries, threats, concerns, troubles, and fears. How many of these would be included in the word "all" that Paul used above? You love God because you are reading books like this to better understand His Word. We read above that *all things work together for good to them that love God who are the called according to his purpose.* So, what is God's will or His purpose to which Paul refers? He answers that question in a letter to Timothy. 1 Timothy 2:3-4:

> **3 For this is good and acceptable in the sight of God our Saviour; 4 <u>Who will have all men to be saved, and to come unto the knowledge of the truth.</u>**

So, whether you are studying God's Word to increase your knowledge of the truth or to teach others, you are within His purpose! For God desires that *everyone* be saved and come to the knowledge of the truth–God's Word.

The Christian walk does not come without challenges. In the same way that Paul's struggles turn to benefit his cause, he mentions teachers of the Word who teach for the wrong reasons. Those who are good teachers will teach as an outpouring of Christ from their hearts. However, there are others who preach for profit and self-aggrandizement. What is Paul's opinion on this? Philippians 1:15-18:

> 15 **Some indeed preach Christ even of envy and strife; and some also of good will:** 16 **The one preach[es] Christ [out] of contention, not sincerely, supposing to add affliction to my bonds:**

> 17 **But the other [preaches out] of love, knowing that I am set for the defence of the gospel.** 18 **What then? notwithstanding, [in] every way, whether in pretence, or in truth, Christ is preached; and I therein do rejoice, yea, and will rejoice.**

Whether out of good or bad intentions, Jesus Christ is preached. In that, Paul rejoices and will rejoice.

From the following text, it appears Paul is aware his time on earth will soon be coming to an end. His conviction remains the same: that in all things Christ be glorified! He writes this to his dear friends that, in his life and in his death, Christ may be magnified. Verses 19-20:

> 19 **For I know that this shall turn to my**

salvation through your prayer, and the supply of the Spirit of Jesus Christ,

20 According to my earnest expectation and my hope, that in nothing I shall be ashamed, but that with all boldness, as always, so now also Christ shall be magnified in my body, whether it be by life, or by death.

Paul expresses confidence that his eternal salvation is secured *in Christ*. It is this perspective that allows him to write the following. Verses 21-22:

21 For to me to live is Christ, and [therefore] to die is gain. 22 But if I live in the flesh, this is the fruit of my labour: yet what I shall choose I wot [know] not.

He has a conundrum. If he dies, then he will be with Christ forever which for him is gain. However, if he lives, then he can continue to make known the Gospel of Grace and encourage other grace believers. Verses 23-26:

23 For I am in a strait betwixt [between] two, having a desire to depart, and to be with Christ; which is far better:

24 Nevertheless to abide in the flesh is more needful for you. **25** And having this confidence, I know that I shall abide and continue with you all for your furtherance and joy of faith;

26 That your rejoicing may be more abundant in Jesus Christ for me by my coming to you again.

He wants the Philippians to be filled with rejoicing when he comes to see them again.

He desires their rejoicing be the result of their unity in the Spirit; their singular commitment to faith in the Gospel of Christ. Verses 27:

27 Only let your conversation [manner of living] be as it becometh the gospel of Christ: that whether I come and see you, or else be absent [from you], I may hear of your affairs, that ye stand fast in one spirit, with one mind striving together for the faith of the gospel;

Let us put the last two verses into plain words. They could be stated this way. "Live your life in a way that is fitting for one who is saved by the Gospel of Grace. Whether I am with you or not, stand fast in one spirit and be of one mind. Work together for the belief in the gospel!"

Unfortunately, most churches place their efforts on increasing attendance and bringing in more money. They justify the increase in money will allow them to expand their programs. Not many emphasize the preaching and teaching of the Word of God. Friend, there is no better way for you to learn the Bible than to do what you are doing right now. By reading and studying it, verse-by-verse with the help of the Spirit, you will increase your understanding of the wisdom of God.

Paul mentions his trials and tribulation above which, in the end, serve to glorify God and further His gospel. He is his desire that the Philippians not allow their adversaries to terrify them. Below, the word *perdition* means *total loss or utter destruction.* Verse 28:

> 28 **And in nothing [be] terrified by your adversaries: which is to them an evident token of [their coming] perdition, but to you [a token] of salvation, and that of God.**

Of these earthly trials and tribulations, Paul writes this explanation. Like Christ Who suffered here on earth, we too are to suffer for His sake. Paul himself is our pattern or example. Verses 29-30:

> 29 **For unto you it is given in the behalf of Christ, not only to believe on him, but also to suffer for his sake; 30 Having the same conflict which ye saw in me, and now hear to be in me.**

When it comes to our earthly trials and tribulations, we must endure. We should not be terrified by any works of the enemies. Their actions are the evidence of their future judgement. However, as for us, our faith and persistence in the gospel are the evidence of our salvation which is from God.

3

Philippians 2

The opening verses of this chapter are a continuation of the theme in Philippians 1. We know we are to endure earthly trials and tribulations. We also know the enemies of God, in due time, will suffer His judgment. However, for now, we must press on. We must hold fast the Word of God. We must be of one Spirit. We must be of one mind as we work together to be ambassadors of reconciliation through the Gospel of the Grace of God! Paul writes to the Corinthians concerning our ministry or mission. 2 Corinthians 5:18-19:

> 18 **And all things are of God, who hath reconciled us to himself by Jesus Christ, and <u>hath given to us the ministry of reconciliation</u>; 19 To wit, that God was in Christ, reconciling the world unto himself, not imputing their trespasses unto**

them; and <u>hath committed unto us the word of reconciliation</u>.

By our sharing and teaching the Gospel of Grace, which is *the word of reconciliation*, God is reconciling the world to Himself through Jesus Christ. That is to be the only outward purpose of grace believers.

Paul, speaking with tenderness to those he loves, begins with words of encouragement. By *consolation* he means *the act of comforting or lightening misery or distress of mind*. Usually, the second runner-up receives a consolation prize. This is to console them for not being first. It also means *refreshing the mind or spirit*. 2 Philippians 1:1-2:

> 1 **If there be therefore any <u>consolation in Christ</u>, if any comfort of love, if any fellowship of the Spirit, if any bowels and mercies,**
>
> 2 **[Then] Fulfil ye my joy, that ye be [1] likeminded, [2] having the same love, [3] being of one accord, [4] of one mind.**

A family doctor might state, "If the body is healthy, then everything should be working together optimally."

Paul makes the same statement. When the Body of Christ is healthy, it will be likeminded, filled with the same love, in unity, and singularly minded. How can we be of one mind? There is only one possible way. Each member must have the mind of Christ. Stop for a moment and think about this. How can a group of people have the mind of Christ? Is that even possible? We know that Jesus is the Word of God made flesh. In order for us to know *His* wants, *His* purpose, and *His* plans of us, we must all know *His Word*—the Bible.

There is usually division in any group of people. Some people want this; some want that. Paul continues by listing what should not divide us. Verses 3-4:

> 3 **Let nothing be done through strife or vainglory [pridefulness]; but in lowliness of mind let each [of you] esteem [the] other better than themselves.**

> 4 **Look [focus] not every man on his own things, but every man also on the things of others.**

We should not argue with others or be filled with pride. We are to be humble and consider the needs of others as well as our own. We do this in putting on *the mind of Christ* — by *knowing His Word*. Paul continues in verse 5:

> 5 **Let this mind be in you, which was also in Christ Jesus:**

In putting on the mind of Christ, we are to think like Jesus Christ. We are to walk or act like Him according to the *Word of God*.

Some non-believers might ask us, "Who is this Jesus that we should act like Him?" Here is Paul's response. Verse 6-8:

> 6 **Who, being in the form of God, thought it not robbery to be equal with God:** 7 **But made himself of no reputation, and took upon him the form of a servant, and was made in the likeness of men:** 8 **And being found in fashion as a man, he humbled himself, and became obedient unto death, even the death of the cross.**

This is what God Himself did for us through Christ. Why? So that we, who were once without hope, might be saved. Salvation came at a heavy cost. God gave His only Son. The Lord Jesus Christ is equal to God. All the members of the trinity are equal for there is only one God. Jesus Christ put aside His equality with God and became flesh for us. Being made in the likeness of men. God became flesh and dwelt among men. Christ humbled Himself, thinking not of Himself . . . but thinking of others. His obedience to the will of God the Father was tested to the point of death on the Cross. Christ fulfilled God's requirements for righteousness. Therefore, God raised Him from the dead. Friend, this is a testament to both Christ's righteousness and God's power of resurrection to save!

So, for what purpose did God have Christ do this? Yes, He did this for salvation of believers, but we will see there is something much bigger being accomplished. Verses 9-11:

> 9 **Wherefore God also hath highly exalted him, and given him a name which is above every name:**
>
> 10 **That at the name of Jesus every knee should bow, of things in heaven, and things in earth, and things under the earth;**
>
> 11 **And that every tongue should confess that Jesus Christ is Lord, to the glory of God the Father.**

This is speaking of the glorified Christ—the Risen Savior! God is restoring Creation and reconciling His Creation to Himself. In another letter, Paul explains God's greater purpose. Ephesians 1:10:

> 10 **That in the dispensation of the fulness of times <u>he might gather together in one all things in Christ</u>, both which are in heaven, and which are on earth; even in him:**

Paul writes about this to the Romans and puts it in perspective. It all ties into the final judgment and restoration. Romans 14:11:

> 11 **For it is written, As I live, saith the Lord, every knee shall bow to me, and every tongue shall confess to God.**

In addition to confessing that Jesus Christ is Lord, everyone shall confess their sins. God will make Christ the Judge over all people. There are two reasons why He is singularly suited for this. First, He alone is righteous and free from sin. Therefore, He is the only One worthy. Second, judgment usually comes from a jury of our peers. Christ is God Who became flesh like us. These are the reasons the Lord Jesus Christ alone is suitable for judging all. 2 Timothy 4:1:

1 . . . the Lord Jesus Christ, who shall judge the quick and the dead at his appearing and his kingdom;

Paul is speaking of His Second Coming at the end of the Tribulation when He establishes His earthly Kingdom. This will be the fulfillment of the promises made to those following Peter and the Gospel of the Kingdom. However, grace believers who follow Paul's Gospel of Grace are the Body of Christ. They will be removed or raptured at *His Calling* when He appears and He calls them to Himself before the Tribulation begins.

Now, let us return to our text where Paul is speaking to his beloved friends. Philippians 2:12-13:

12 Wherefore, my beloved, as ye [you all] have always obeyed, not as in my presence only, but now much more in my absence, work out your own salvation with fear and trembling.

13 For it is God which worketh in you both to will and to do of his good pleasure.

We must consider these words *work out your own salvation with fear and trembling*. This is not contrary to

31

Paul's teaching of salvation by grace, through faith, and without works. We know we are expected *to act worthy of our calling*. However, our salvation is secured in Christ. Paul is referring to our conversation or manner of living while we wait for *His Calling*.

Let us consider this. Our salvation has been bought and paid for by Christ's blood. Salvation becomes effective immediately upon the moment we believe the Gospel of Grace. His death, burial, and resurrection are sufficient for salvation. Nothing can be added. Why? It is because of Christ's righteousness; not ours. God imparts His righteousness to those who believe. It is not our own righteousness and it is certainly not earned by our works. Once saved, we are spiritually in Christ Who is in heaven, but physically we are here on earth in the flesh. So, when will our bodies be redeemed?

In his letter to the Ephesians, Paul explains the current state of grace believers. Ephesians 1:13-14:

> 13 **In whom [God] ye also trusted, after that ye heard the word of truth, the gospel of your salvation: in whom also after that ye believed, ye were sealed with that holy Spirit of promise,**
>
> 14 **Which [Who] is the earnest of our in-**

heritance until the redemption of the purchased possession, unto the praise of his glory.

We learn we are saved the moment we believe the Gospel of Grace. We immediately are placed spiritually *in Christ.* However, we physically remain on earth until *His calling* which is the Rapture. To guaranty the fulfillment of the purchase God gives each believer the *holy Spirit of Promise.* This is the *earnest* or *deposit* that secures or guarantees the completion of our redemption. We are saved. We have salvation, but physically God has chosen to leave us on earth to fulfill His purpose. Therefore, the word *salvation,* in the above verse, would imply *our current state of salvation while awaiting its fulfillment.* There is no jeopardy of losing your salvation.

With this in view, what does Paul mean by *working out our own salvation with fear and trembling?* This is tied to the desire he expressed in Philippians 1:27:

> **27 Only let your conversation [manner of living] be as it becometh the gospel of Christ . . . that ye stand fast in one spirit, with one mind striving together for the faith of the gospel;**

For those who love God, the word *fear* can mean *respect*. When we fear someone who loves us, it really is respect. To this end: while we are here on earth awaiting *His calling*, we are to work or act accordingly. During our sojourn here, we are to respect God as we consider the terrible judgment to come—not of us, but of the world who rejects Him.

He continues his teaching on our *conversation* or our *manner of living*. Philippians 2:14-15:

> 14 **Do all things without murmurings and disputings:**
>
> 15 **That ye may be blameless and harmless, the sons of God, without rebuke, in the midst of a crooked and perverse nation, among whom ye shine as lights in the world;**

We are not to complain or argue with each other. Our affairs while on earth are to be above reproach. In another letter, he speaks about the current state of the world as well as our need to put on the mind of Christ. Romans 12:2:

> 2 **And be not conformed to this world: but be ye transformed by the renewing of your mind, that ye may prove what is**

that good, and acceptable, and perfect, will of God.

We are not to follow the ways of the world. Instead, we are to be transformed or changed. How are we to be changed? It is by the renewing of our mind. How are we to do that? When we read the Bible and study His Word, we take on *the mind of Christ*. That is how we *renew our mind*.

The Word of God will transform our mind, but it is also the hope of salvation for those who are not saved. Those who are saved must consider those who are not remembering that while we were still sinners, Christ died for us. Romans 10:14-15:

> **14 How then shall they call on him in whom they have not believed? and how shall they believe in him of whom they have not heard? and how shall they hear without a preacher?**
>
> **15 And how shall they preach, except they be sent? as it is written, How beautiful are the feet of them that preach the gospel of peace, and bring glad tidings of good things!**

Only those who have heard and believed the Gospel

of Grace can tell those who have not heard. Paul is asking a valid question: How can anyone believe in Him of Whom they have not heard? Believers, those who first believe, must make the message of salvation to those who have not heard. Paul says that he can rejoice at *the day of Christ*, which is the Rapture, knowing that his work was not without fruit. Philippians 2:16:

> **16 Holding forth the word of life; that I may rejoice in the day of Christ, that I have not run in vain, neither laboured in vain.**

Those for whom he labored are those that believed. It was his desire that they would share the message of grace with others and, by so doing, Paul will not have labored in vain.

He mentions the uncertainty of his trial and his hopes to see his beloved Philippians again. His dedication to the Gospel of Grace and his care towards those who believed are his sacrifices to God. Verses 17-18:

> **17 Yea, and if I be offered upon the sacrifice and service of your faith, I joy, and rejoice with you all.**

18 For the same cause also do ye joy, and rejoice with me.

Paul did not minister alone. He had Timothy and Titus who were teachers as well as others who helped him. Some would write his letters for him, due to his eye problems, and deliver these letters as a courier. He writes concerning Timothy in verses 19-20:

19 But I trust in the Lord Jesus to send Timotheus shortly unto you, that I also may be of good comfort, when I know your state.

20 For I have no man likeminded, who will naturally care for your state. **21** For all seek their own, not the things which are Jesus Christ's.

Continuing, he refers to Timothy and their relationship being similar to a father and son in their ministry. Verses 22-24:

22 But ye know the proof of him, that, as a son with the father, he [Timothy] hath served with me in the gospel.

23 Him therefore I hope to send [to you] presently, so soon as [until] I shall see how it will go with me. 24 But I trust in the Lord that I also myself shall come [to you] shortly.

Epaphroditus will travel to Philippi with this letter in which he will not only deliver the letter to them, but also provide news of Paul's life and ministry. Verse 25:

25 Yet I supposed [believed] it necessary to send to you Epaphroditus, my brother, and companion in labour, and fellowsoldier, but [now] your messenger, and he that ministered [here] to my wants.

News had reached the Philippians concerning Epaphroditus' illness which brought him close to death and they were distraught. Verses 26-30:

26 For he longed after you all, and was full of heaviness, because that ye had heard that he had been sick. 27 For indeed he was sick nigh unto death: but God had mercy on him; and not on him only, but on me also, lest I should have sorrow upon sorrow.

28 I sent him therefore the more care-

fully, that, when ye see him again, ye may rejoice, and that I may be the less sorrowful.

29 Receive him therefore in the Lord with all gladness; and hold such in reputation:

30 Because for the work of Christ he was nigh unto death, not regarding his life, to supply your lack of service toward me.

It is evident that Epaphroditus was deeply committed to the saints and cared greatly for them. With his health having been restored, Paul choose him to travel to Philippi on his behalf with this letter.

4

Philippians 3

In spite of every challenge, Paul wants the Philippians to be filled with joy. He knows there is evil in the world and wolves seek to devour the children of light. Therefore, he wants to encourage them to look beyond this. Philippians 3:1:

1 Finally, my brethren, rejoice in the Lord. To write the same things to you, to me indeed is not grievous, but for you it is safe.

To tell them what he has told others is not burdensome because he is doing it for their safety. He proceeds to warn them of whom they should be aware. Speaking of those who trouble them, he writes in verses 2-3:

2 Beware of dogs, beware of evil work-

ers, beware of the concision [Jews]. 3 For we are the [true] circumcision, which worship God in the spirit, and rejoice in Christ Jesus, and have no confidence in the flesh.

He uses the word *dogs* to refer to the unsaved and do evil. He mentions another group. The word *concision* comes from the Greek word meaning *mutilation*. These are the zealous Jews who follow the Law religiously and glory in their flesh. Some pious Jews bothered the grace believers insisting they be circumcised and follow the Law of Moses. For Jews, this was required of the Law and they falsely taught it was necessary for the Gentiles' salvation.

This act or work of the flesh is contrary to Paul's Gospel of Grace. These particular Jews wanted to glory by getting those saved by grace to be circumcised. Here is what Paul wrote to the Galatians who were being troubled by those under the Law. Galatians 6:14-15

14 But God forbid that I should glory, save [except] in the cross of our Lord Jesus Christ, by whom the world is crucified unto me, and I unto the world.

15 For in Christ Jesus neither [does] cir-

cumcision availeth [achieve] any thing, nor [does] uncircumcision, but [we are] a new creature [in Christ].

The difference becomes clearer as one studies Paul's teaching. The Gospel of the Kingdom requires the fulfillment of the Law. Paul writes this in Romans 15:8:

> 8 Now I say that Jesus Christ was a minister of the circumcision for the truth of God, to confirm the promises made unto the fathers:

Speaking at the Jewish holiday called Festival of the Firstfruits, also called Pentecost, the Apostle Peter answered a question. Acts 2:37-38:

> 37 Now when they heard this, they were pricked in their heart, and said unto Peter and to the rest of the apostles, <u>Men and brethren, what shall we do?</u>

> 38 Then Peter said unto them, <u>Repent, and be baptized every one of you in the name of Jesus Christ for the remission of sins</u>, and ye shall receive the gift of the Holy Ghost.

Did you notice the result of repentance and baptism is *remission* of sins. This is not the same as *forgiveness.* For the Jews will receive their forgiveness when their Messiah returns. How are they to act until then? Christ gives His instructions to His eleven apostles at His Ascension. Matthew 28:18-20:

> 18 **And Jesus came and spake unto them [His apostles], saying, All power is given unto me in heaven and in earth.**
>
> 19 **Go ye therefore, and teach all nations, baptizing them in the name of the Father, and of the Son, and of the Holy Ghost: 20 Teaching them to observe all things whatsoever I have commanded you: and, lo, I am with you alway, even unto the end of the world. Amen.**

Those Jews saved under the Gospel of the Kingdom must continue to observe the Law. Until when? Until He returns for them at the end of the Tribulation.

As you can see, this is different than the Gospel of Grace which is solely dependent upon faith in Christ's righteousness and God's gift of that righteousness to those who believe. By comparing his own perfection under the Law, Paul makes this point clear. If we were to have certainty in the acts of the flesh, then no one could be more confident than he. Philippians 3:4-6:

> **4 Though I [myself] might also have confidence in the flesh. If any other man thinketh that he hath [confidence] whereof he might trust in the flesh, I more:**

> **5 Circumcised the eighth day, of the stock of Israel, of the tribe of Benjamin, an Hebrew of the Hebrews; as touching [concerning] the law, a Pharisee;**

> **6 Concerning zeal, persecuting the church; touching the righteousness which is in the law, blameless.**

Paul is saying that if anyone should be able to boast in the flesh, as these Jews who were bothering the new believers were, then he could exceed their boasting.

He now compares his former life to the life he now has in Christ. Verses 7-9:

> **7 But what things were gain to me [then], those [things] I counted loss for Christ.**

8 Yea doubtless, and I count all things but loss for the excellency of the knowledge of Christ Jesus my Lord: for whom I have suffered the loss of all things, and do count them but dung [manure], that I may win Christ,

9 And be [being] found in him [in Christ], <u>not having mine own right-eousness, which is of the law, but that which is through the faith of Christ, the righteousness which is of God by faith</u>:

Paul's future, before his conversion on the Road to Damascus, was as a rising star in the Jewish religion. Concerning the Law and traditions, he was flawless. When he compares that to his knowledge of his Lord Jesus Christ, he counts the former as manure. This side-by-side comparison brings these differences more to light. Paul no longer seeks righteousness of himself from the Law. Instead, he acknowledges receiving the righteousness of Christ through faith which is a gift of God. My friend, it is critical to your understanding of Scripture to see the difference between the Gospel of the Kingdom and Paul's Gospel of Grace.

Concerning this gift of grace offered by God, he speaks personally of the impact it had upon him.

Verses 10-11:

> 10 That I may know him, and the power of his resurrection, and the fellowship of his sufferings, being made conformable unto his death;

> 11 If by any means I might attain unto the resurrection of the dead.

Paul acknowledges his own imperfection and the impossibility to achieve it, by any means, on his own. Yet, he presses on towards the goal. Verses 12-14:

> 12 Not as though I had already attained, either were already perfect: but I follow after, if that I may apprehend that for which also I am apprehended of Christ Jesus.

> 13 Brethren, I count not myself to have apprehended [understood] [all things]: but this one thing I do, [1] forgetting those things which are behind, and [2] reaching forth unto those things which are before,

> 14 I press toward the mark for the prize of the high calling of God in Christ

Jesus.

These above verses are important to understand but require a bit of unpacking. He chooses to use the word *apprehend* to mean *fully or completely understand.*

If we read it again and replace the word *apprehend* with the word *understand*, it becomes clearer. Paul admits he is not perfect. Still, he pursues Christ in order to gain a deeper understanding of Him. He tell us there is one thing he does understand. By forgetting the things which are behind him, his past, he can now choose to reach for those things which are before him. These would be the promises of our completed redemption in *His Calling.* Like Paul, we must put aside our past. Now, having the righteousness of Christ, we must choose to focus on the things to come. Doing this, we can press on towards *the prize.* You may ask, "What is *this prize?*" Paul provides the answer in verse 14. The *prize* is *the high Calling of God in Christ Jesus*–the Rapture!

Let us reflect for a moment. Look at the words *the high calling of God in Christ Jesus.* Paul's teaching on this concept is important. I may interpret this differently than others, but the remainder of the chapter will bear proof if I am correct. I do not believe that Paul is speaking about what many refer to as ministerial callings. In Ephesians, Paul states these ministries are gifts or abilities which God *gives* to individuals. They are for the purpose of edifying the Body of Christ while we sojourn here on earth. (See Eph. 4:11-12.)

There is another *calling* which *all* grace believers will receive. In fact, it is guaranteed to be a part of their future. It is their inheritance which is *in Christ*. Ephesians 1:18:

> 18 **The eyes of your understanding being enlightened; that ye may know what is <u>the hope of his calling,</u> and what <u>the riches of the glory of his inheritance in the saints,</u>**

His Calling will be the completion of our redemption which is the fulfillment of the promise. Our bodily redemption happens at *His Calling* – the Rapture. Paul writes about this to Timothy and ties it in with our afflictions during our earthly sojourn. 2 Timothy 1:8-9:

> 8 **Be not thou therefore ashamed of the testimony of our Lord, nor of me his prisoner: but <u>be thou partaker of the afflictions of the gospel according to the power of God;</u>**

49

9 Who hath saved us, and called us with an holy calling, not according to our works, but according to his own purpose and grace, which was given [to] us in Christ Jesus before the world began

This interpretation is consistent with Paul's prayer for the Ephesians and, for that matter, all grace believers. Remember, those who are saved by grace are perfect in God's sight not with their own righteousness, but with the righteousness of Christ. Ephesians 1:17-18:

17 That the God of our Lord Jesus Christ, the Father of glory, may give unto you the spirit of wisdom and revelation in the knowledge of him:

18 The eyes of your understanding being enlightened; that ye may know what is the hope of his calling, and what the riches of the glory of his inheritance in the saints,

Our inheritance, our *blessed hope,* is the appearance of the Lord Jesus Christ and *His calling* of His church unto Himself. Titus 2:13:

13 Looking for that blessed hope, and

<u>the glorious appearing of the great God
and our Saviour Jesus Christ;</u>

My friend, be confident of this. Our *blessed hope* is the
Rapture! Therefore, *forgetting those things which are be-
hind us, reach forth unto those things which are before us.*
And, then what? Press on toward the mark, the finish
line, for the prize of the high calling of God in Christ
Jesus. (See Phil. 3:13-14.)

Returning to our text, Paul draws a conclusion
from the preceding. Philippians 3:15-16:

**15 Let us therefore, as many as be per-
fect, be thus minded: and if in any thing
ye be otherwise minded, God shall reveal even this unto you. 16 Nevertheless,
whereto we have already attained, let us
walk by the same rule, let us mind the
same thing.**

Paul is referring to those of us who have taken on the
righteousness or perfection of Christ. That is an act
of God in which He imparts Christ's righteousness to
grace believers. He directs them to be *thus minded.* In
other words, *think this way* and God will reveal this
to you. See what we have already received, salvation
by the grace of God! Now, being able to see this, we
should walk or live by this same knowledge. God has

saved us and declared us righteous in Christ. We should, therefore, be like-minded. You may ask, "How are we to do this?"

Many Christians think Paul is boastful. I would have to disagree, especially in later life. He is very direct in his teaching and he should be. His teaching is a matter of eternal importance. He learned humility through his sufferings for the gospel. It may surprise some Christians to learn that Paul was the first to be saved by grace. We will confirm that momentarily. This was for good reason because Paul would become the example or patten by which God showed His grace. 1 Timothy 1:15-16:

> 15 **This is a faithful saying, and worthy of all acceptation, that Christ Jesus came into the world to save sinners; of whom I am chief.** 16 **Howbeit for this cause I obtained mercy, that in me first Jesus Christ might shew forth all longsuffering, for a pattern to them which should hereafter believe on him to life everlasting.**

God saved Paul for this very reason. Paul admits he was the chief of sinners, the worst of the worst, because he persecuted the church. Think about this. If God could save the worst of the worst, then He could certainly save anyone, right? God saved Paul so that he could be *a pattern*. A *pattern* is an *example* or a *pro-type* for those that follow. The Gospel of Grace is more powerful because the man who proclaims this gospel to others is the first to testify to its effectiveness.

He continues with Philippians 3:17:

17 Brethren, be followers together of me, and mark [notice] them which walk so as ye have us for an ensample.

Scripture tells us Paul is our pattern or protype. We are to follow him. He is our example. Before you reject this thought, you must ask, "Why is that?" His sole focus remained unchanged–to follow Christ. As grace believers, we are to follow Paul's example. We are to follow Christ!

He adds a parenthetical comment warning believers against fakes and deceivers. Verses 18-19:

18 (For many walk, of whom I have told you often, and now tell you even weeping, that they are the enemies of the cross of Christ:

19 Whose end is destruction, whose God

is their belly, and whose glory is in their shame, who mind earthly things.)

He is imploring those saved by grace, to the point of tears, that they must be vigilant. There are many who appear to be of them, but they are not. Allow me to paraphrase these words: *whose god is their belly and whose self-glory is in their shame.* Their carnal desires are to advance their self-interests both materially, through their belly, and pridefully, through self-glory.

Remember this. We are sojourners or aliens in a foreign land. We are *in the world*, but *not of the world*. We are to be holy which means separated from the world. We belong to God. Our *conversation* or *manner of living* is in heaven which is our destiny *in Christ*. Keep looking upwards. Verse 20:

20 For our conversation is in heaven; from whence [what place] also we look for the Saviour, the Lord Jesus Christ:

We are temporarily on earth, but our future is in heaven with Christ. Here, Paul returns to our *blessed hope* described above — *His Calling.* What will happen when the Lord Jesus Christ calls us away? Verse 21:

21 Who shall change our vile body, that

it may be fashioned like unto his glorious body, according to the working whereby he is able even to subdue all things unto himself.

5

Philippians 4

As we approach the end of Paul's letter, you will sense his love for these grace believers. They had listened to his teaching while he was with them. In his absence, they had made his instruction part of their daily manner of living. The Philippians were a source of great encouragement to him. Philippians 4:1:

> 1 **Therefore, my brethren dearly beloved and longed for, my joy and crown, so stand fast in the Lord, my dearly beloved.**

He had received news of certain individuals whom he knew and felt comfortable giving them individual instruction. Verses 2-3:

> 2 **I beseech Euodias, and beseech Syn-**

tyche, that they be of the same mind in the Lord.

3 And I intreat thee also, true yokefellow, help those women which laboured with me in the gospel, with Clement also, and with other my fellow-labourers, whose names are in the book of life.

This is proof of Paul's intimate knowledge of these individuals in Philippi. This is much the same way in which teachers know the students in their classroom.

Paul wants to leave them with words of preparation and encouragement. He offers his instruction on how to deal with adversity. For he also was experiencing hardship. The conclusion of this letter is similar to that of another. To the grace believers in Ephesus, he instructed them to put on the whole armor of God for their defense. (See Eph. 6:10-8.) To the Philippians, he writes to them that they should continue in their joy, as should we. Verse 4:

4 Rejoice in the Lord alway: and again I say, Rejoice.

This applies to all grace believers. We should rejoice and be filled with joy in the Lord. Who would not want this? He explains how they can do that. We should not diminish this because of its simplicity.

He sets the stage by putting everything into the context of daily living. Verse 5:

> 5 **Let your moderation be known unto all men. The Lord is at hand.**

First, it is easier for a person of moderation to rejoice than someone who is not. The more we have of material possessions and position, the more we are under pressure to conform to the world. Second, we must remember the hope of *His Calling* which is imminent.

As humans, we are subject to our emotions. In the following verse, the word *careful* does not hold its current meaning of *being cautious*. Here, the words *careful* literally means *being filled with care*. In other words, he is saying for us to *be anxious for nothing* or *do not be filled with care about anything!* Verse 6:

> 6 **Be careful for nothing; but in every thing by prayer and supplication with thanksgiving let your requests be made known unto God.**

We must understand that we are *in Christ* and what

that means for us. Our relationship with God is intimate. He knows us personally. He knows what we need before we even ask. However, He wants us to talk with Him about *everything!* Prayer is talking with God. When we talk with Him, we are to make our requests known. As we do this, we must also remember to thank Him for Who He is, what He has done for us, and what He has given us. By giving thanks, it confirms our faith of Who God is and that He hears our prayers.

Making requests to God must be done in faith. When we hit a brick wall and there seems to be no solution, as grace believers we have an incredible blessing! We can turn to Him. Later, in the Epilogue, I will share with you some tools I use in counseling. When we turn our cares over to Him, truly turn them over, that means we are giving them to Him. We are transferring them to Someone much more capable to deal with the problems.

When I hit a problem beyond my ability, I like to think of it as being above my pay grade. In other words, I turn it over to Someone Who knows how to deal with the problem. I am learning to transfer the problem to God knowing it is now in more capable hands. I try not to worry about it any longer. Give the problem to God and believe that He will handle it. That is faith in action. Do we believe God heard out request? Do we believe that God is capable of handling our problem? Taking our problem back, when we have already given it to God, is not putting our faith in action. This is what Paul wrote in Ephesians 3:20:

> 20 Now <u>unto him that is able to do ex-ceeding abundantly above all that we ask or think</u>, according to the power that worketh in us,

God hears our concerns and He is able to respond in a way that is above what we ask or think. We must trust Him!

By doing this, it becomes our source of joy and peace. See how Paul describes it. Philippians 4:7:

> 7 And the peace of God, which passeth all understanding, shall keep your hearts and minds through Christ Jesus.

Fear and anxiety wreak havoc on two things: our hearts, which are our emotion, and our minds, which are our thoughts. Paul is someone well experienced in adversity and he is telling us the result is a peace that is beyond our comprehension. Jesus Christ will keep our hearts and minds safely *in Him*.

Assume we are able to transfer our problems to God and then put into action our faith by trusting Him. What shall we do with all the extra time we used to spend worrying and fretting? With this new-found peace of mind, what shall we do? Since we are no longer being consumed by cares, we can devote it to fortifying our new minds. Paul tells us this shall keep, or guard, *our hearts and minds* through Christ Jesus (v. 7). How can we do this? Verse 8:

> 8 **Finally, brethren, . . .**
> **whatsoever things are <u>true</u>,**
> **whatsoever things are <u>honest</u>,**
> **whatsoever things are <u>just</u>,**
> **whatsoever things are <u>pure</u>,**
> **whatsoever things are <u>lovely</u>,**
> **whatsoever things are <u>of good report</u>;**
> **if there be <u>any virtue</u>, and**
> **if there be <u>any praise</u>,**
> **<u>think on these things</u>.**

I arranged this as a list to make Paul's point very clear. Alleviated from our cares and concerns, we are to set our thoughts on those things from above. We must make it our goal to avoid negativity, complaining, or focusing our mind on things not of God. They will deplete our hope and our joy. However, concentrating on things which are good, things which are from God, will fortify our hearts, and minds–our emotions and our thoughts

Paul reminds us that he is our example. Regardless of his struggles, failings, trials, and tribulations, he never took his eyes off the eternal prize. What is this prize? It is Christ in us the hope of glory. Paul dedicated his life to preaching the Gospel of Grace and caring for grace believers. Verse 9:

> 9 **Those things, which ye have both learned, and received, and heard, and seen in me, do: and the God of peace shall be with you.**

I would like to restate the above verse with more emphasis. If all the things you learned from me, received from me, and heard from me, and seen me do, you do also, then the God of peace shall also be with you. Throughout Paul's life, he had learned to put his concept into action. He is telling us to emulate him and, if we do, we will have the peace of God which he also has.

He expresses his gratitude to the Philippians for their support for both him personally as well as for the needs of his ministry. In the following, the word *careful* means *to be full of care or concerning*. In other words, *anxious*. Verse 10:

10 But I rejoiced in the Lord greatly, that now at the last [in these recent days] your care of me hath flourished again; wherein ye were also careful, but ye lacked opportunity.

He is not making known any needs, but tells them that in whatever state he finds himself, he is content. Verse 11:

11 Not that I speak in respect of want: for I have learned, in whatsoever state I am, therewith to be content.

Most people are unaware of the sufferings Paul endured throughout his apostleship. It may have more of a dramatic impact if we pause for a moment to consider them. It will give you a better understanding of Paul who is as a minister of the Gospel of the Grace of God. Here is a list he writes in 2 Corinthians 11:23-24

23 Are they ministers of Christ? (I speak as a fool) I am more; in labours more abundant, in stripes [injury by beatings] above measure, in prisons more frequent, in deaths oft. **24** Of the Jews five times received I forty stripes save one.

The Jews believed that flogging or beating a man with forty stripes would kill him. So, they beat him thirty-nine times which was one short of death. We continue with verses 25-26:

> 25 Thrice was I beaten with rods, once was I stoned, thrice I suffered shipwreck, a night and a day I have been in the deep [stranded in the sea]; 26 In journeyings often, in perils of waters, in perils of robbers, in perils by mine own countrymen, in perils by the heathen, in perils in the city, in perils in the wilderness, in perils in the sea, in perils among false brethren;

The above is a list of perils he experienced. However, what about his needs and his emotions? Verses 27-29:

> 27 In weariness and painfulness, in watchings often, in hunger and thirst, in fastings often, in cold and nakedness. 28 Beside those things that are without, that which cometh upon me daily, the care of all the churches. 29 Who is weak, and I am not weak? who is offended, and I burn not?

From this, Paul came to the realization of this truth. We will finish this with verses 30-31:

> 30 **If I must needs [have] glory, I will glory of [in] the things which concern mine infirmities.** 31 **The God and Father of our Lord Jesus Christ, which is blessed for evermore, knoweth that I lie not.**

In view of the above history, let us now return to Philippians 4:12-13:

> 12 **I know both how to be abased [suffer need], and I know how to abound [have plenty]: every where and in all things I am instructed both to be full and to be hungry, both to abound and to suffer need.**

> 13 **I can do all things through Christ which strengtheneth me.**

This is one of Paul's most well-known verses of encouragement. To tie this together, it may help if we look back at Philippians verse 1:11:

> 11 **Being filled with the fruits of righteousness, which are by [from] Jesus**

Christ, unto the glory and praise of God.

I think there is a theme here. So, our good works which Paul calls the fruits of righteousness are through, by, or from Jesus Christ. Verse 4:13 above tells us the same thing. When things get difficult, when things get too hard, or when we do not know what to do, we have this thought to lean upon. Jesus Christ is our source of strength. We can do all things with the strength we receive through, by, or from Him.

This is the same strength that Paul depended upon for his own trials and tribulation. God had used the believers in Philippi to provide for his needs. It is this generosity he now acknowledges. He tells them *notwithstanding* meaning *in spite of the circumstances.* Philippians 4:14-15:

> 14 **Notwithstanding ye have well done, that ye did communicate with my affliction.**
>
> 15 **Now ye Philippians know also, that in the beginning of [my sharing] the gospel, when I departed from Macedonia, no church communicated with me**

**as concerning giving and receiving, but
ye only.**

When Paul moved on from one group of believers to another, we learn it was only the Philippians who kept in touch with him. From what little they had, they continued to provide for his needs. Verses 16-18:

> 16 **For even in Thessalonica ye sent once and again unto my necessity. 17 Not because I desire a gift: but I desire fruit that may abound to your account.**
>
> 18 **But I have all, and abound: I am full, having received of Epaphroditus the things which were sent from you, an odour of a sweet smell, a sacrifice acceptable, wellpleasing to God.**

He is grateful for their commitment and generosity. Knowing what we do, the fruit we produce, we do it because we are his workmanship. Our good works were ordained by God that we should walk in them. They were created in Christ Jesus. (See Eph. 2:10.) In order to complete these works which were determined or ordained by God, we must have the strength to do them. That strength we receive through Him. God assures us of this in verses 19-20:

19 But my God shall supply all your need according to his riches in glory by Christ Jesus.

20 Now unto God and our Father be glory for ever and ever. Amen.

Paul completes this letter by sending greetings to all the saints. His letters are read aloud in the congregation. He mentions those who are in his company while writing the letter. They send their greetings to their fellow grace believers in Philippi. Verse 21:

21 Salute [Greet] every saint in Christ Jesus. The brethren which are with me greet you.

22 All the saints salute you, chiefly they that are of Caesar's household.

To the grace believers who would first hear this letter read aloud, and to those grace believers who will subsequently read this letter almost two thousand years later, Paul writes this blessing. Verse 23:

23 The grace of our Lord Jesus Christ be with you all. Amen.

Epilogue

I promised to share a counseling tool I use. It helps people who are dealing with anxiety. We may think, in view of current events, we are more susceptible to being filled with care and worry than those living during Paul's time. I think not. Evil existed before Adam. Nothing has changed. Although it may be more blatantly visible today. However, it has been there all the time and will continue to grow especially after *His Calling*–the Rapture.

Today, we are no different than the Philippian grace believers to whom Paul was writing his letter. His desire for them as well as all grace believers is that they be filled with joy because of what the Lord had done for them. Notice what comes first. Philippians 4:4:

4 Rejoice in the Lord alway: and again I say, Rejoice.

If someone was to ask the question, "How can we do this in such a time as this?" Let us look closely at his instructions and then we will put them into practical use. Philippians 4:6:

> 6 **Be careful for nothing; but in every thing by prayer and supplication with thanksgiving let your requests be made known unto God.**

In plain terms, he starts by telling them, in order to be filled with joy, first, they must not be filled with cares. Do not worry, then he continues with what we should do. Instead, we are to talk with God . . . about everything! That means both the small stuff and the big stuff. If it is something that concerns us, then we must commit it to prayer.

Many of us tell our friends or fellow believers all our woes and cares, but we do not tell God. Perhaps it is because we believe He already knows. Having told someone our problems, for some reason we feel better just having shared it with someone else. Why is that wrong? Most of the time we are dumping our problems, cares, and concerns onto someone else who does not have the power to fix them. Think about it. We may feel better by sharing our woes, but we have just unloaded our problems onto someone else, again, who is unable to solve our problems.

By turning over or transferring our problems, cares, concerns to Someone Who is able to handle them, we are doing something. Our friends who listen to us whine and complain cannot. We cannot transfer our problems to them. However, we can transfer them to God. Hold on a minute! Paul is telling us not to dump our problems on others, but to bring them to God. Yes, then, he tells us the reason why in verse 7.

7 And the peace of God, which passeth all understanding, shall keep your hearts and minds through Christ Jesus.

If we give our problems to God and, most importantly, then we trust Him, in both His wisdom and power, to solve them. Would that not be reason enough for us to be filled with joy? For many it would be a sufficient reason to rejoice!

Paul continues in the following verses to explain what I call "the invisible force field," but only we can activate it. In view of our geopolitical environment, who would not want one of those? Allow me to give a personal example. We hear many people discussing current events. They are appalled at the actions of some people, yet they dwell on them. They fixate on them and seem to enjoy sharing these atrocities with anyone who will listen. I stop them midsentence. I admit that I cannot solve these problems. However, I know from Paul's teaching that I can protect my heart and my mind. These would be my emotions and my thoughts. We are to do this in order to "... *keep our hearts and minds through Christ Jesus.*"

Does this work? It absolutely does. Here is why. So, what am I talking about when I call it an *invisible forcefield?* Paul gives us details on this *forcefield.* Its purpose is to ... *keep our hearts and minds through Christ Jesus.*" The key to using this forcefield is turning it on, putting it into action, and using it to protect our heart and mind. Philippians 4:8:

> 8 **Finally, brethren,**
> **whatsoever things are true,**
> **whatsoever things are honest,**
> **whatsoever things are just,**
> **whatsoever things are pure,**
> **whatsoever things are lovely,**
> **whatsoever things are of good report;**
> **if there be any virtue,**
> **and if there be any praise,**
> **think on these things.**

When we receive bad news, negativity, hatred, or anger, we get a sick feeling in the pit of our stomach.

Our spirit cringing from such thoughts. However, it is our choice how we will react. We can, once again, focus our thoughts and emotions on whatever we choose. It is like riding a horse or being on a diet. If we fall off, then get right back on!

In view of the list above, Paul tells us to focus on the good. Find those who are like-minded and encourage each other to do the same. Verse 9:

> 9 **Those things, which ye have both learned, and received, and heard, and seen in [from] me, [you need to] do: and the God of peace shall be with you.**

Fellowship with others who are saved by grace because together we can put into practice those things which were taught and done by Paul. Strive always to share with others the good and pleasant things we see and do.

I am an ordained Christian counselor. Counseling, for me, is pointing to Christ and His Word. Not only is He the solution, but there is no greater Counselor Who knows us better inside and out. Sharing relevant Scripture with my clients, I encourage them to put this into action. To make it fun and easy, I developed a counseling tool which is broken down into five steps.

I hold up my hand with an open palm. This is universally understood to mean *Stop!* They need to stop what they are doing and think. Next, with my hand raised, I wiggle my five fingers. It is a bit theatrical, but it helps them to remember there are five steps or stages in the process. As we progress, my fingers are folded down, one at a time, as we move through the process. We will follow Paul's instructions by using this overly simplified tool.

Most people can relate to these five steps or stages and I encourage them to adapt them to their own individual needs. Before I begin, I always confirm they believe and accepting God's gracious offer of salvation by grace without works is a prerequisite. It is our acceptance of this that puts us, as grace believers, in a unique relationship with God. It places us *in Christ.* Positionally, we are *in Christ* spiritually. However, physically we remain on earth in the flesh and it is our flesh which is the temporary cause of our problems.

Having our position *in Christ,* God does not see our sinfulness. He sees the righteousness of Christ which He imparts to those who believe. Our access to God is not limited as we have the same access as His Son. Before we start, I am figuratively holding up the palm of my hand. Stop for a moment and think about that. When we are in trouble and need help, we have access to the Creator of the Universe. We are to be full of care or anxious for nothing!

The first step is easy. We must start by acknowledging our problem or concern is beyond our ability to handle. What may be a problem for you may not be a problem for someone else. Therefore, this is something personal and is between you and God. As we move through the stages, we will find this to be an exercise of faith. It is putting our faith into action. With all that Paul went through, he finally learned what to do. He wants us to follow his example–to do what we do. So, he was speaking from experience and wants to save us from the hardship of learning this lesson on our own. Therefore, for our sakes, we should follow his example.

➢ **First, acknowledge we have a problem or concern that is beyond our ability.**

Having a problem that we are unable to handle can be both frustrating and frightening. We can *in everything by prayer and supplication with thanksgiving let our requests be made known unto God*. The problem is no longer ours. We need to transfer it to God Who is "able to do exceeding abundantly above all that we ask or think" (Eph. 3:20).

Think of transferring something as handing something over to someone else. By doing this, we no longer have the problem to solve. Yes, we are still "in" the problem, but its solution is now in the hands of Almighty God. Initially, we gave the problem to God because we believe His Word. Taking the problem back upon our shoulders would be a lack of trust and faith in the Person to Whom we gave this problem, would it not?

The second stage is realizing that the problem is no longer ours. Life must continue even if we must live within the problem. It is more of a sense that the problem no longer belongs to us. We trust the Someone Who is going to solve it. Do not take the problem back! Remember, we transferred it to God. We must realize that God works in His time; not ours. He is more than aware of all the factors at play. I would summarize this step as follows:

> ➢ **Second, remember this. We have given the problem to God. Do not take it back! Instead, have faith in Him. We must trust Him. Believe He will answer your prayer.**

This stage is the most difficult because it tests our faith that God heard us and that He will answer the requests of those He loves. Think of it this way. We are saved and, according to Ephesians, we are

In Christ. Now, picture Jesus Christ asking His Father for something. What are the chances God will hear and answer His request? Of course, any request must be consistent with His will. We can pray for world peace, and it will happen, but not until the end. If we want to build our faith, then start by asking for something personal, even if it is for someone else.

The next step is about recognizing God as being omniscient, all-knowing, and omnipotence, all-powerful. When we transfer our problem and put it in His hands, we must allow Him to provide the best answer or solution. He knows the circumstances. Therefore, He may not answer our prayer or solve our problem in a way we want. I think this stage involves two things. First, we must trust Him to provide us with the best solution. Second, it is a matter of acceptance. Like any father who has the best interest of his child, God can choose to answer with either a "no" or a "not now." We must accept that Our Father knows best and He wants what is best for us.

Accepting can be difficult. I was teaching and a student was very angry at God. She had prayed repeatedly for the healing of her husband who had cancer. She told me that God never answered her prayer. We talked for a while and I told her that He did answer her prayer, He said "no." God is not arbitrary or capricious. He always makes His decisions based upon His perfect will. It is part of His sovereignty since God has the final decision. If God should say "no" in response to our request, we must not turn away from Him in anger. Instead, we need to ask Him the reason why and show us why He said "no." He will let us know the reason.

During this stage, continue to pray and talk to Him. We should not pray in repetition, but instead ask God to open our eyes and ears to see Him moving in our life. Sometimes, an opportunity or door may open. We must see that and participate in the solution, but always moving in prayer. It may be part of the process just ask Him. This is the same God Who parted the Red Sea for Moses; yet once parted, Israel had to walk by their own initiative across on the dry ground. They saw the miracle, but they needed to walk through the waters. He Who raised the Lord Jesus Christ from the dead is the One working on our behalf. We definitely do not want to miss seeing His hand moving in our life. Exercising our faith begets faith in the same way that using muscles builds muscles.

➢ **Third, continue in faith. Having asked, believe God heard the request! Our relationship with God must be based upon faith. He will respond. Should He say "no" to the request,**

ask Him why. Do not miss seeing God move! Have eyes of faith. Be watchful. Allow Him to be the Sovereign God. He chooses how to handle the problem according to His will and has our best interest at heart.

Stage three is the most difficult. We must be patient while we exercise our faith. Wait for His answer as you continue to pray throughout this whole process. A key component to our prayers is being thanksgiving. Thanking God for what He has already done for you and others builds our faith. So, remember to thank Him. Picture an ungrateful child who approaches her father to ask for something more. Now, picture another child who is always grateful. When she approaches her father, the reception of her request might be viewed differently.

When God answers our prayer or provides a solution to our problem, regardless of how He does it, we must be grateful. It is difficult not to become emotional when we see the Creator of the Universe, Who cares enough about us as an individual, to solve our dilemma. With eyes of faith, we can see this. To any father, the love and gratitude of a thankful child is always welcome. Our God is our Father and we should be His grateful children. Sometimes, we might find that throughout the process God was teaching us or molding us. It is part of the sanctifying process we go through while waiting for *His Calling*.

> ➢ **Fourth, remember to thank Him! Tell Him what you learned.**

We are thankful to Him and must always remember His gracious love and faithfulness to us.

I suggest one more step. This step, along with our gratitude, should never end. No one can refute a personal testimony. Eyewitness testimony is the personal recollection of the events which someone saw. Our story may build someone's faith in God.

> ➢ **Fifth, tell others about what God has done for you.**

It builds up other believers and non-believers as well. It achieves what Paul desires for every assembly. He wants all grace believers to rejoice and be filled with joy. The only way to do this is by having an active relationship with God. We must talk to Him regularly, not just when we are in a sinking boat. Thank Him for what He has done. Rejoice! Be filled with joy knowing that we can confidently bring our requests to Him at any time. Encourage others to do the same.

Paul gives this wonderful benediction to grace believers in Ephesians 3:20-21:

> 20 **Now unto him that is able to do exceeding abundantly above all that we ask or think, according to the power that worketh in us,**
>
> 21 **Unto him be glory in the church by Christ Jesus throughout all ages, world without end. Amen.**

—Dr. David Alan Greene

Other GraceWord Publications

In English:

1st Corinthians: Dispensationally Considered
1st & 2nd Thessalonians: Dispensationally Con.
1st & 2nd Timothy & Titus: Dispensationally Con.
2nd Corinthians: Dispensationally Considered
Acts: Dispensationally Considered
Colossians & Philemon: Dispensationally Con.
Ephesians: Dispensationally Considered
Galatians: Dispensationally Considered
Hebrews: Dispensationally Considered
How Am I Wired?
Letters To Theophilus
Philippians: Dispensationally Considered
Romans: Dispensationally Considered
The Glorious Destiny Of Israel
The Hidden Gospel
The Seven Hebrew Epistles: Dispensationally Con.
Two Distinct Gospel Messages Of The New Test.

En español:

Cartas A Teófilo
Efesios: Dispensacionalmente considerado
El evangelio Oculto: Una vez fue un misterio . . .

About The Author

Dr. David Alan Greene has over thirty-five years of experience as an insurance agent selling both property and casualty as well as life insurance. During his career, he taught and explained the content and meaning of policies to his clients. Now retired, he devotes much of his time to teaching the Bible.

He received his Bachelor of Theology, Master of Biblical Studies, and Ph.D. in Biblical Studies from Evangelical Theological Seminary where he holds the position of Dean of Graduate Studies. He also holds a Ph.D. in Christian Counseling. He has written numerous biblical commentaries and books on rightly dividing the Word of Truth.

www.ingramcontent.com/pod-product-compliance
Lightning Source LLC
Chambersburg PA
CBHW070758120626
46557CB00002B/650